# GUAM
## A Natural History

## SKILLS BOOK

Dr. Ann Rayson

BESS PRESS

3565 Harding Avenue  Honolulu, Hawai'i  96816
(808) 734-7159  Fax (808) 732-3627  www.besspress.com

# Contents

# CHAPTER 1    The Birth of Guam

## READING SKILLS

A geologist is a scientist who studies _____. Geologists have studied Guam for over _____ years. They found that 50 million years ago there were no _____ in this part of the Pacific. But sections of _____ moved. These sections are called _____. They _____ or _____ over a layer of warm soft _____ below. When rock is melted, this underground _____ is called _____.

About 45 to 50 _____ years ago, the _____ and the Philippine Plate _____ together. This formed an underwater _____. Melted _____ came up through cracks in the _____ Plate. The rock spread out and formed _____. These plates still rub together and cause _____ and _____. Where these two plates meet, the _____ formed.

The island of Guam began nearly _____ million years ago in the _____ Age, when the earth was still _____. Strange _____ roamed the land. The first _____ appeared, but there were no _____. The _____ passed under the _____ Plate. _____ erupted underwater and _____ poured into the sea. Some of the magma formed part of Guam's "_____" rocks. Once above the _____, the new island grew quickly. A _____ grew on the shores.

The Eocene age came to an end and the Northwest _____ disappeared.

The next age, the _____, began 38 million years ago and lasted for _____ years. A major _____ in the area that is now Guam forced Guam's "basement" rocks above sea level. The other _____ Islands were formed this way too. The new islands formed an island arc. The next period, the _____, began 23 million years ago and lasted for _____million years. _____ spread across the continents, and herds of _____ roamed the plains. _____ still took place in the Pacific. _____ moved up and down. Then _____ activity stopped about _____ million years ago. The highest part of Guam was _____. That is why there is _____ on top of some mountains.

The _____ age began _____ million years ago and ended two million years ago. The first _____ appeared on earth in _____. The _____ age started almost two million years ago. This is sometimes called The _____ Age. _____ bridges appeared between _____ and Alaska, and between North and South _____. Each time the ice melted, the _____ rose. Guam moved below and above _____ during this time. An _____ pushed the reef above sea level _____. The Philippine _____ moved up. This formed Guam's northern _____. It is a valuable source of _____ and _____. From limestone we get _____to build roads.

Before the 1950s, people thought Guam was once a _____. There is a new _____ about Guam now. Maybe Guam formed south of the _____ because the Philippine Plate is slowly _____.

## MATCH THE AGES OF THE EARTH:

| | |
|---|---|
| Eocene | The Ice Age |
| Miocene | lasted 15 million years |
| Oligocene | Guam began |
| Pleistocene | the first people appeared |
| Pliocene | began 23 million years ago |

## MATCHING: Match the word with the description.

| | |
|---|---|
| lava | underground lava |
| magma | melted rock |
| Marianas Arc | layers of coral reef |
| Marianas Trench | sections of the Earth's crust |
| plates | chain of volcanoes |
| terrraces | seven miles deep |

## DO YOU KNOW?

1. What is the Mariana Trench?_____

_____

_____


2. What happened to the two volcanoes that made Guam?_____

_____

_____

3. Why is northern Guam different from southern Guam? _____

_____

_____

4. Why are there "sea caves" high up in Guam's cliffs today? _____

_____

_____

5. How old is Guam? _____

_____

## THINGS TO DO:

1. Find a fossil.

2. Visit an ancient reef.

3. Find some limestone.

4. Make a map of how the world looked during the Ice Age.

# CHAPTER 2    The Land

**READING SKILLS:**

Guam lies north of the _____ and east of the prime meridian.

Guam is in the tropics between the _____ and

_____. It lies _____ of the International

Date Line. When it's Sunday in the United States, it is _____ in Guam.

Old folks say Guam formed from the body of a _____. Its island

is thirty miles long from _____ Point to _____.

It is _____ miles wide from _____ Point to

_____ Bay. It is only _____ miles wide between

_____ Bay and _____ Bay. There are

_____ square miles of land on Guam. The two halves of the island were

formed in different _____ at different _____.

Later they _____.

The northern half is a wide limestone _____ with steep

_____. It is _____ feet high in the northeast and slopes

down to 200 feet near the _____ of Guam. _____ formed

the plateau when Guam was _____ in the _____

period. The reefs formed on top of _____. The old coral reefs turned

to _____ at least _____ million years ago.

If you dig down into it, the color is _____. Much of the Mariana

Limestone has pieces of _____ coral that turned to _____.

A thin layer of reddish _____ covers most of the Mariana Limestone.

This is Guam _____. It gets its red color from _____.

There are no real _____ in northern Guam. Limestone is like a

_____. Water makes limestone _____ to form

underground _____. All of Guam's limestone _____

have caves in them. The _____ are some of the best caves. The

ancient _____ used these, and _____ sol-

diers hid in them during and after _____. Northern Guam is full of

_____ made when _____ fall in. When _____

sinks through limestone, it comes out at sea level. It forms _____

around the edges of northern Guam.

Southern Guam is rolling _____ land. It has a few _____

and several high volcanic _____. The oldest peaks are _____,

_____, and _____. Their volcanic rock is

from the _____ period, _____ million years ago.

The highest of the ridges is on the _____ coast _____

of the first ridge. You can see this ridge along the road from _____

to _____.

The _____ mountain range starts near Umatac and stretches to

_____. Mt. _____ is in a Guam legend.

You can see volcanic rock along the _____ Road. One kind is

_____ lava. Another kind of lava is _____.

It is the _____ rock full of tiny _____.

Some beaches in southern Guam are made of _____. It is

_____ than white coral sand and is called _____ sand.

It is from the mineral _____. At Cetti Bay and Merizo Bay there is

another dark sand called _____ sand. It is made from the mineral

_____.

The rainwater in Guam forms streams and _____. The largest

river system is the _____. The United States _____

made a large lake in the _____ Valley by damming the river

there. The Guam government built a _____ on the

_____ River. Many people get their _____

from these dams.

    The _____ River and the _____ River

are two other large streams. The _____ River in Central Guam

comes out of the ground at Agana _____. It flows out to

_____.

    The rivers of southern Guam drop over cliffs, making _____.

_____ Falls is one of the best known. It is on the

_____ River. A little falls is the _____. It is

on the _____ River. _____ Falls is near the

Cross Island Road. The highest falls drops _____ feet into a pool. One of

Guam's highest is _____ Falls near Mt. _____.

It drops _____ feet. _____ live in these pools,

and people like to _____ in them.

    The maritime tropical zones have two seasons, a _____ and a

_____. Guam's rainy season lasts from _____

through _____. The dry season is from _____

through _____. Annual rainfal is from _____

to _____ inches. During the dry season Guam has a pleasant climate

because _____ blow constantly. The average temperature on

Guam is _____, the same as the _____.

All year the temperature stays between _____ and _____.

Some years it is _____ and there is a water _____.

Then brush _____ may start. During the rainy season the

_____ winds blow. Tropical _____ bring most of the rain in the rainy _____. _____ are Guam's strongest cyclones. They are known for very strong _____. _____ is one of Guam's worst typhoon months. Since _____ many people have built typhoon-proof homes and buildings. They use _____ with _____ inside.

Guam is a high point on an _____. Sometimes the _____ slips up or down along the _____ Trench. Then there is an _____ on Guam. Two underwater volcanic _____ to the west of Guam sometimes cause earthquakes. Scientists use a _____ to track earthquakes. They are measured on a _____ scale. An earthquake of _____ or higher usually causes damage. Since 1900 almost _____ earthquakes hit the Mariana Islands. All were over _____ in strength.

A better name for tidal waves is _____. They are _____, _____ waves caused by _____. The _____ Islands have had terrible _____. Guam has not had as many. In _____ a tidal wave rushed into _____ and washed a woman out to sea. The 1993 earthquake caused a _____.

## MATCHING PUZZLE: Match the word with the description.

| | |
|---|---|
| cyclones | off the road to Ritidian |
| 1953 | Ylig River |
| large sinkholes | rotating storms |
| Talofofo | blows in the rainy season |
| Sumongsong | blow during the dry season |
| tidal wave | "big wind" in Chinese |
| Tarzan Falls | "stay-in-the-village time" |
| Southwest Monsoon | Typhoon Alice |
| typhoon | records shocks |
| tsunamis | tsunami |
| Northeast Trade Winds | strong, fast waves caused by earthquakes |
| seismograph | largest river system on Guam |

## DO YOU KNOW?

1. What are latitude and longitude? What is Guam's map location?

2. Tell the story of the giant who lay on his back to make Guam. (See *A History of Guam*.)

3. What should you do when you feel an earthquake?

## THINGS TO DO:

1. Visit a black sand beach and a green sand beach.

2. Bring in some pumice lava.

3. Go look at some pillow lava.

4. Interview someone who experienced a recent typhoon or earthquake. Report to the class.

# CHAPTER 3     The Plants

**MULTIPLE CHOICE:**

1. Most seashore plants came to Guam by _____.

   a. fish

   b. boats

   c. floating

   d. birds


2. _____ carried many jungle plants to Guam.

   a. lizards

   b. storms

   c. winds

   d. birds


3. The _____ carried a few plants to Guam.

   a. wind

   b. sea

   c. Spanish

   d. monkeys


4. Today there are _____ species of plants on Guam. _____ of these are trees.

   a. 500-100

   b. 900-200

   c. 80-20

   d. 300-50

5. _____This vine helps hold beach soil together.

    a. papaya

    b. swordgrass

    c. goatsfoot

    d. ironwood


## Vocabulary: DO YOU KNOW THESE WORDS?

DEFINE each word and use each word in a sentence:

reproduce_____

_____

microscope_____

_____

species_____

_____

savannas_____

_____

plantain_____

_____

spores_____

_____

cultivated_____

_____

boondocks_____

_____

lavender_____

_____

approve_____

_____

mysterious_____

_____

strangle_____

_____

prop_____

_____

introduced_____

_____

## MATCHING: TREES

1. _____ This tree was used as a fish poison.

2. _____ Some people think these trees are haunted.

3. _____ This tree has fruit the size of a head.

4. _____ This tree was used for house posts and cartwheels.

5. _____ In early days, this was the most important tree to the Chamorros.

6. _____ The nuts of this tree are poisonous.

7. _____ People make clocks of this.

8. _____ People still make baskets from this tree.

9. _____ In the old days, people made its bark into rope.

10. _____ Caterpillers love this tree.

**ANSWERS:** banyan, barringtonia, breadfruit, coconut, federico, flame tree, ifil, palo maria, pandanus, wild hibiscus

## MATCHING: PLANTS

1. _____ This plant was used for copra.

2. _____ People used to eat this plant and build houses with it.

3. _____ This plant has lavender flowers.

4. _____ This plant is sometimes called "boondocks."

5. _____ This plant can cut skin like a razor.

6. _____ Its leaves can cure skin diseases.

7. _____ This tastes like a melon.

**ANSWERS:** bamboo, candlebush, coconut, goatsfoot vine, hedge acacia, papaya, swordgrass

# PUZZLE: DRAW LINES TO THE CORRECT ANSWERS

Who brought these plants to Guam?

candlebush

The Spanish                    flame tree

banana

hedge acacia

The Early Chamorros            seedless breadfruit

papaya

## SHORT ESSAYS:

1. What plants came to Guam from Mexico? Who brought them to Guam?

2. What did the ancient Chamorros use the coconut palm for? There were many uses.

## DO SOME RESEARCH:

Where did these plants come from? Plumeria, vanda orchid, hibiscus, corn, sweet potato, pineapple. You can name other plants on Guam and then try to find out where they came from and who brought them to Guam.

## THINGS TO DO:

1. Collect as many plant leaves as you can from your yard or neighborhood. Dry them and glue them to sheets of paper. Make these sheets into a book.

2. Make collage pictures of seeds you collect from different plants.

3. Make a chart of plant and tree uses.

4. Make flashcards from heavy paper with English plant names on one side and Chamorro plant names on the other side. Take turns testing each other on both names for each plant.

5. Look at color slides of plants from your resource center.

6. Look at leaves and seeds under a microscope.

## OTHER RESOURCES:

ANCIENT CHAMORRO SOCIETY, by Lawrence J. Cunningham. Honolulu: Bess Press, 1992.

ATLAS OF MICRONESIA, by Bruce G. Karolle. Honolulu: Bess Press, 1993.

THE CHAMORRO WORD BOOK, by Marilyn Salas. Honolulu: Bess Press, 1998.

GUAM PAST AND PRESENT, by Charles Beardsley. Tokyo: Charles E. Tuttle Co., 1964.

HAWAIIAN FLOWERS AND FLOWERING TREES, by Loraine E. Kuck and Richard C. Tongg. Tokyo: Charles E. Tuttle Co., 1960.

PACIFIC ISLAND BATTLEGROUNDS of WORLD WAR II: THEN AND NOW, by Earl Hinz. Honolulu: Bess Press, 1995.

PACIFIC NATIONS AND TERRITORIES, Third Edition, by Reilly Ridgell. Honolulu: Bess Press, 1995.

PACIFIC NEIGHBORS: THE ISLANDS OF MICRONESIA, MELANESIA, AND POLYNESIA, by Betty Dunford and Reilly Ridgell. Honolulu: Bess Press, 1996.

PLANT LIFE OF THE PACIFIC WORLD, by Elmer D. Merrill. New York: MacMillan, 1945.

# CHAPTER 4    Animals of the Land

**FILL IN THE BLANK:**

1. The only native mammal in Guam is the _____.

2. The smallest lizard on Guam is the _____.

3. These creatures eat geckos: _____.

4. These wild animals are welcome in houses: _____.

5. A full moon brings the _____ out.

6. _____ kinds of skinks live on Guam. (how many?)

7. People brought the pests _____ and _____

   to Guam.

8. The _____ is Guam's largest native lizard.

9. The little _____ snake has been on Guam for many years.

10. Wild pigs usually have _____ baby pigs. (how many?)

11. Governor _____ brought the _____ to

Guam from _____ between 1771 and 1774.

12. The village of _____ has _____ races and

   _____ games.

13. _____ like to eat rat poison!

14. Now the _____ eats Guam's snails.

15. On Guam you can hunt _____ with a license.

**VOCABULARY: Do you know the meanings of these words? Define and use each in a sentence.**

1. roost_____

_____

2. excitedly_____

_____

3. extinct_____

_____

4. endangered_____

_____

5. buck_____

_____

6. doe_____

_____

7. poacher_____

_____

8. fertilize_____

_____

9. cannibal_____

_____

**PUZZLE: Draw lines to show which animals are endangered and which are good to eat.**

fruit bat

endangered

coconut crab

land crab

good to eat

many skinks

some geckos

**WORD SKILLS: Draw a line from the English name to the Chamorro name for these animals.**

| | |
|---|---|
| blind-snake | *achi'ak* |
| brown tree snake | *akaleha'* |
| carabao/water buffalo | *ayuyu* |
| coconut crab | *babuen hålomtåno* |
| fruit bat | *binådu* |
| gecko | *chå'ka* |
| giant African snail | *fanihi* |
| giant toad | *guåli'ek* |
| Guam deer | *iguana/hilitai* |
| land crab | *karabao* |
| monitor lizard | *kulepbla* |
| rats/mice/shrews | *panglao tano'* |
| skinks/moles | *tot* |
| wild pig | *ulo' åttelong* |

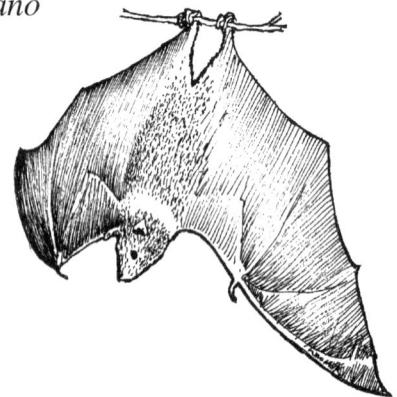

18

## PUZZLE: Match the animal with who brought it to Guam or where it came from.

Spanish

Americans

Japanese

Papua New Guinea

African snail

brown tree snake

carabao

house mouse

Norway rat

pigs

roof rat

shrew

toads

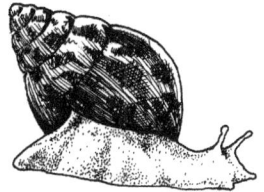

## SHORT ESSAYS:

1. How did the first animals come to Guam? _____

_____

_____

2. Why is the fruit bat called a "flying fox"? _____

_____

_____

3. Why are *ayuyu* called "robber crabs"? _____

_____

_____

4. How do *chả'ka* cause trouble?_____

_____

_____


5. Describe the monitor lizard. Have you ever seen one?_____

_____

_____


6. Why don't farmers like wild pigs?_____

_____

_____


7. Why are Guam deer called "barking deer"_____

_____

_____


8. What are the rules for deer hunting on Guam?_____

_____

_____


9. What work did carabao used to do on Guam?_____

_____

_____


10. Why did the government brings toads to Guam?_____

_____

_____

11. You should not handle toads because _____

_____

_____


12. African snails are pests because _____

_____

_____


12. Why is it dangerous to bring a new animal to an island?_____

_____

_____


13. What animal is Guam's biggest problem? Why?_____

_____

_____

## ACTIVITIES

1. Get a snake trap from the DAWR. If you catch a brown tree snake, take it to the DAWR for scientists to study.

2. Visit the Department of Agriculture, Fish and Wildlife Division.

3. Make a map showing where Guam's animals come from.

4. Collect tadpoles and watch them hatch.

5. Draw pictures of Guam's animals.

6. Make flashcards from heavy paper. Put the English name of each animal on Guam on one side and the Chamorro name for each animal on the other side. Take turns quizzing each other on the names.

# CHAPTER 5    Guam's Birds

## NATIVE LAND BIRDS

There aren't many _____ on Guam because the _____

killed most of them. It eats the _____ and young _____.

About _____ different kinds of birds used to nest here. Some visit during

the _____ months. Many live in Guam's _____.

You have to _____ for them.

Guam rails cannot _____. Only _____

has the *ko'ko'*. They lost their power of flight _____ of years ago

because they had no _____. The _____

is trying to save the *ko'ko'*. It lays up to _____ eggs in a nest in the

_____. In 1996 there were _____ *ko'ko'* in captivity.

The yellow bittern, or_____, is a _____

flyer. It nests in _____ or _____ and lays

_____ white eggs.

The Mariana fruit dove, or _____, was one of the most

_____ birds on Guam. It has not been found on Guam since _____.

Few people ever see the tottot because of its _____ color. Scientists

think the fruit dove came from _____ thousands of years ago.

No one has seen the _____ on Guam since 1987. It nests in

_____ trees like the _____. Flocks of

_____ used to fly around above the _____.

In 1996 there were just _____ on Guam. They could become _____.

They live in _____ and make _____ noises.

In other Asian countries people boil their _____ for soup.

The _____ disappeared from Guam in 1986. Again,

the _____ is responsible. The *egigi* likes _____

and _____ flowers. It has a _____ bill to

drink _____ and is found in _____.

Since 1988 you cannot find the _____ in the wild. In 1996,

_____ were in captivity. _____ scientists are trying to

save this bird. It swoops down on _____ , _____,

and small _____. It kills insect _____.

But many people did not like the _____ because it

_____.

One of three birds on Guam called a "blackbird" is the _____.

The *sali* does not damage _____ or _____

and likes to eat _____ and _____. It is also

in danger and threatened by the _____. In 1996 there were only

_____ left on Guam.

The second blackbird is the _____, found only on Guam and

_____. In 1996 there were only _____ on

Guam. They lay eggs, but the eggs don't _____.

The _____ was last seen on Guam in the late 1960s.

Three things killed it: 1)_____, 2)_____,

and 3) _____. The snake seems to be only on _____

and _____. The chichirika, a little _____, is also

no longer on Guam. It disappeared in 1984 because of the _____.

This bird is a _____catcher. The rufous fantail is found in the southern

_____ and _____.

The _____ is gone forever. No one has seen it since _____ ,

and we blame the _____. This bird was found only on

_____. Scientists think they first came from _____.

The _____ was the smallest of Guam's jungle birds. They

became _____ on Guam in 1984 because of the _____.

Some other birds visit Guam by _____. An example is called

the _____ in Chamorro. The early Chamorros killed off a large

_____ and a small _____.

## NATIVE WATER BIRDS

The _____ is a seabird of Guam's highest _____.

Now _____ are rare on Guam. The smallest white seabird, the

_____, is seen most often around _____

trees on Guam. Terns do not make a _____, but lay an egg on a

_____ of a tree. They live on tiny _____

and _____. Most terns are on _____.

The _____ is a dark brown tern that nests on Guam's

_____. It skims along the water and _____

fish and squid.

The _____ is a large seabird twice the size

of a _____. They fish by _____.

_____ like seabirds because they lead them to _____.

The _____ comes in _____ colors.

They have _____ legs and _____. Usually

they nest on _____ off Guam.

You will see the _____ only in freshwater marshes or

_____. In _____ only 100-200 were left on

Guam. It is sometimes known as a "_____."

The _____ was one of the rare birds of the world and was Guam's only native _____. Scientists last saw *ngånga'* in Guam in _____. They caught the last three on _____ in 1979. Now they are gone forever.

## BIRDS BROUGHT BY HUMANS

In 1894 Captain _____ brought the _____ to Guam from the Philippines for _____. They would rather _____ than fly. A Spanish official brought the _____ from the _____ in the 1770s. Today it is common in _____ areas. The _____ is the common _____ of city parks. It was brought to Guam in early _____ days as a _____ bird and now is found _____. Some people _____ them.

A visitor brought the _____ and let his birds go when he left Guam in the _____. The large flocks are now probably _____. About the same time, the _____ came after 1945. Today it is _____ all over the island. It survives the _____. Guam's third "blackbird" is the _____. It has a very long _____. Its bill has a _____. Drongos came to Guam from _____ in the _____. In 1935 the _____ took them from Taiwan to _____ to eat _____ pests. Other birds brought to Guam _____ out. The Department of Agriculture brought _____ from Indian in 1961. They can be _____.

Other birds visit Guam when they _____. Most of them are _____ birds. Three of these are the: 1) _____, 2) _____, and 3) _____.

**MATCHING PUZZLE on The Brown Tree Snake:**

1. bridled white-eye

2. common moorhen

3. Guam flycatcher

4. Guam rail

Wiped out by brown tree snake:      5. island swiftlet

6. Mariana crow

7. Mariana fruit dove

_____      8. Mariana mallard

9. Micronesian honey-eater

Threatened by brown tree snake:      10. Micronesian kingfisher

11. Micronesian starling

12. nightingale reed-warbler

_____      13. rufous fantail

## DO YOU KNOW?

1. How did the Guam rail lose its power to fly? How did it get its colors? (You can read the story in _A History of Guam._)

_____

_____

_____

_____

2. What jungle bird is green? _____

3. What Guam bird is sometimes mistaken for a bat?_____

4. How did the bengbeng (painted quail) get its name?_____

_____


5. What bird came to Guam from Rota?_____


6. Why don't the Mariana crows' eggs hatch?_____

_____


7. How did the booby get its name?_____


8. How does the tree sparrow survive the brown tree snake?_____

_____


9. How does the drongo avoid the brown tree snake?_____

_____


**THINGS TO DO:**

1. Make drawings of Guam's birds.

2. Take a bird walk and see what birds you can find.

3. Make a map showing bird migration to Guam.

# CHAPTER 6    Animals of the Sea

## CORALS

_____ ring the shores of Guam. Tumoge Reef is around

_____. _____ was once around Apra Harbor,

a _____. Coral grows best in _____water.

It needs an underwater shelf of _____ or the side of an

_____ to grow on. Fresh _____ stops coral

from _____.

Tiny animals called _____ build the reef. They take _____

out of the seawater and make them into stony _____. The polyps live inside

their skeletons in tiny _____. They feed on _____

at night.

There are many kinds of _____. _____ is

one of the most common. You will see it at _____. Alive it is a

_____ color. It is rough and can _____ you.

_____ coral looks like a _____ brain. Some

are _____ and others are pink. _____ grow

into coral heads. There are many heads in _____. One coral has a

_____ skeleton. Scientists call it _____. You

can find it below _____. _____ coral

grows in flat yellow leaves. If you touch it, it will _____ you.

_____ coral is different from all the others. It starts on the

_____ of the bay.

## SEA CUCUMBERS

Guam's _____ are full of sea cucumbers. Some people call

them _____. Some are black, some are brown, and some have

_____ dots. They are the earthworms of the sea. If you bother

the sea cucumber, it will _____ and grow new ones. A

sea cucumber can stick to your body like _____. Dried cucumbers

are called _____ and can be used in _____.

Sea _____ have sharp spines that stick out all over. They walk

on their _____ feet that are _____ with

_____ cups. Sea urchins feed on _____.

The best known sea star on Guam is the _____.These animals

are often called _____. They eat _____

matter on the reef. The crown-of-thorns sea star has many _____ and

eats _____.The _____ is the strangest sea star.

## SEASHELLS

Some of the most beautiful _____ in the world can

be found on Guam's _____. You need a permit to collect the

_____. Most of the year it is illegal to catch the _____

called *hima*. People like to _____ *hima*, but can only collect it in

_____.

_____ are round, shiny shells. They hide during the daytime in

_____. In _____ people

used the _____ for money. One of Guam's largest is the

_____ cowrie. It comes out in the _____.

You can find it at _____ Bay. One of Guam's rarest is the

_____ cowrie. It is rare because_____.

Scientists find it off _____.

_____ shells hunt at night and sting their prey

with _____ of the cones are poisonous

to _____, and some could _____

you. _____ are long, slim shells. They hide under

the _____ and come out at _____.

_____ look like tall hats worn by bishops. They live in

_____ and eat _____. The favorite Guam

shell is the _____. It does not _____.

## OTHERS

The _____ is hard to see on the reef because it

can change _____. It will squirt out _____

for a smoke screen, but will not _____ you. It has _____

legs called _____. If you pick one up, it could _____

you. Many kinds of _____ live in Guam's _____.

_____ crabs live in empty _____.

## REEF

The most colorful sea creatures of all are the _____. You can see

them wherever _____ is growing. _____

usually are yellow with black stripes. The _____ has an orange "nose."

The _____ hides in holes and can bite you. The _____

is poisonous if eaten. The cornetfish has a mouth like a _____.

The _____ can puff up its stomach when caught. They can be

_____ to eat. Most squirrel fish are _____

in color with large _____. A cowfish is in the _____

family. It can be _____. The _____ has three

black bands and is easy to _____. The clownfish has _____

on its scales which keeps it from being _____. There are _____

kinds on Guam. One of the strangest reef fish is the _____. It is hard

to tell which _____ is up. The _____ is a silver fish

that lives in _____ at the surface of the _____.

The _____ got its name from prisoners who used to wear

_____ uniforms. The large ones are a favorite _____

on Guam. The most dangerous inner reef fish is the _____. It looks

like a _____, but has _____ poisonous spines on

its back. It can _____ your feet. There are _____ types

of triggerfish on Guam. Sometimes they _____ swimmers. One kind

looks like a _____ painting. _____ are long

and swim in _____. They all have two _____

under their chins called _____ to help them find food in the

_____. The _____ is like a piece of paper.

It can change _____ to match the _____.

The _____ looks like a Christmas tree and lives in a _____.

Sea turtles and sea snakes are _____. They lay

their eggs on _____. All sea turtles are threatened because

_____.

It is _____ to buy any part of a sea turtle. We need to

_____ the reef animals.

## THINGS TO DO:

1. Start a saltwater aquarium.

2. Have a shell collector speak to the class.


**PUZZLE on Reef Fish: Match the name of the fish with its description. Some fish can fit more than one.**


Good in an aquarium:                          cowfish

                                              damselfish

Bad in an aquarium:                           moray eel

                                              reef eel

Can bite you:                                 sharp-nose puffer

                                              small squirrel fish

Can poison you:                               squirrel fish

                                              stonefish

Can sting you:                                tiny convict tang

                                              triggerfish

May eat your aquarium fish:

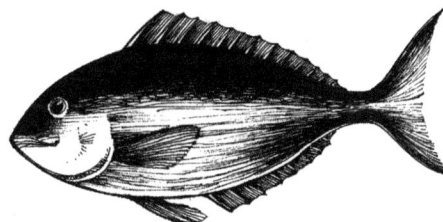

**PUZZLE: Fill in the blank with the correct word for each definition.**

1. _____ Tiny plants and animals afloat in the sea.

2. _____ Soft, flower-like animals.

3. _____ Squirts ink.

4. _____ Squirts its insides out.

5. _____ "Sea porcupines"

6. _____ Starfish

7. _____ You cannot collect over fifty pounds a day.

8. _____ You can only catch in May and June.

9. _____ It is illegal to buy any part.

10. _____ Six of the tropical Pacific ones are poisonous.

11. _____ Children make it come out by saying "duk-duk-duk."

## DO YOU KNOW?

1. What is a coral polyp?_____

_____

2. What sea animal has a fish that lives inside it?_____

3. What shell animals can kill you?_____

4. What fish likes to "stand on its head"?_____

5. Why do goatfish have "whiskers"?_____

_____

6. How did the triggerfish get its name?_____

_____

# CHAPTER 7     Micronesia and Its Pacific Neighbors

**READING SKILLS:**

More than _____ islands are in the Pacific _____.
Europeans put them in three groups: _____,
_____, and _____. Melanesia means
" _____." People there have _____ skins.
These islands include _____, _____,
_____, _____,
_____, and _____.

Polynesia means _____. Its people are
_____ and _____ with straight _____.
Some of these islands are _____, _____,
_____, _____, the Tuamotu
_____, _____,
_____, _____,
_____, _____, and
_____.

_____ means "small islands." Its people are various
_____ speaking peoples. It contains most of the islands in the
_____ north of the _____. Its two islands
with Polynesian people are _____ and _____.
Scientists later found the people of the Pacific could not _____.
Only the _____ were alike and spoke the same _____.

Micronesia and Melanesia had many different groups of people who spoke many different

_____. They _____ different from one

another and had different _____.

    Guam and the Mariana Islands are part of _____.

Other island groups here are the _____, the _____,

and the _____ Islands. Most of these were once part of the

_____ of the Pacific Islands. These were not a part of it:

_____, _____,

and _____. Now the Gilbert Islands are the

_____; _____ is a republic too. The Mariana

Islands except for Guam became the _____.

Some island groups formed the FSM, the _____.

The FSM includes: _____, _____,

_____, and _____. Palau became a

_____. So did the _____. Only people in the

CNMI became U.S. _____. Most people speak their own language

and _____. They use _____ money. The

_____ defends them.

    Micronesia has over _____ islands stretching _____

miles across the ocean. Some high islands are _____. Some low

islands are small, and some are called _____. A coral atoll is a

_____ of narrow islands around a _____.

The largest island in Micronesia is _____. It is _____

square miles. Then comes _____ in Palau. It is _____

square miles. Next is _____ with 129 square miles. Most of the

others are much _____.Guam is important to the Micronesian

islands because it is the _____. The people

of Micronesia get many of their _____ from Guam and come to

Guam for _____ and college. They come to live and _____.

## DO YOU KNOW?

1. For what reasons did Europeans divide the Pacific islands into three groups?_____

_____

_____

2. Why are these divisions no longer useful to scientists?_____

_____

_____

3. Which people are U.S. citizens and why?_____

_____

_____

4. Why is Guam important to the Micronesian islands?_____

_____

_____

# CHAPTER 8    The Mariana Islands

**READING SKILLS:**

Underwater _____ formed the Mariana Islands. Some are still active on the _____ islands. _____ settled the Mariana Islands over _____ years ago. Europeans did not find Guam until _____. After 1565, Spanish _____ stopped here every year. In 1668 the country of _____ settled the Marianas, and from _____ to _____ Spain _____ the Mariana Islands. The _____ won a war against _____ in 1898 and captured _____. It decided to keep Guam as a _____ for its navy. Since it didn't want the other Mariana Islands, _____ sold them to _____. Germany kept them until _____ when it started _____. Then _____ took over Guam's islands in the Pacific and kept them until _____.

The _____ took the Mariana Islands from Japan. The takeover of Guam began on _____. We call it _____. The _____ made the Marianas except _____ part of the Trust Territory of the Pacific Islands with the _____ in charge. In _____ they became self-governing as the _____. They had a constitution and became _____ citizens. In 1990 the UN ended the _____.

In 1995 the CNMI had _____ people, but only _____ were citizens of both the _____ and the _____.

Of these, 20,087 were _____ and _____.

The majority of 32,401 came from other countries, mostly _____.

These people came to work in _____, _____,

_____, and _____. Some _____

and some are _____.

    There are _____ islands in the Mariana Chain, which is _____

miles long. Guam is the farthest _____ and the _____.

Guam remains a territory of the _____ and so is not a part of the

other _____.

    The closest island to Guam is _____, about _____

miles north. It is _____ square miles and _____

feet high. In 1995, _____ people lived there. They speak a purer

_____ language than anywhere else. Rota has a small _____

industry and the largest _____ stones in the Marianas.

    Tiny _____ is about _____ miles north of Rota.

Today _____ lives here. It has less than _____

square miles of land. In _____ the Chamorros fought a brave battle against the

Spanish here. After World War II the military used it for _____.

Scientists used this island as a testing ground to see if _____ snails

would kill the _____. Did they? _____.

Today people go here to hunt _____ and _____.

    Just north of Aguiguan is _____. It has _____

square miles of land. In 1995 it had _____ people. The biggest village

is _____. Most of the island is _____, but

it has some _____ and _____.

The _____ ranch started in 1965. Tinian attracts tourists by

building _____. Americans captured Tinian during _____.

Bombers from here dropped the first _____ on _____ and _____. The _____ has huge latte stones _____ feet tall. Taga was a great _____.

Close to Tinian is _____, the capital of the CNMI. At _____ square miles it is the _____ largest island in the Mariana chain. Its highest mountain is _____ feet tall. The _____ developed Saipan and made _____ a large city. It had many _____ and a _____ line. Saipan was the center of Japanese _____ growing. Saipan and Rota even had _____ to collect the cane. In _____ America captured Saipan from Japan in a very _____ battle. Today many _____ come here. About _____ people live on Saipan, half from _____.

The tiny island of _____ is fifty miles north of Saipan. It is the _____ of the Marianas with only _____ square miles of land made up of _____. Does anyone live here? _____.

_____ is a huge mountain with steep _____. The first _____ island, it rises out of the sea to _____ feet. The _____ in the top has a _____ in it. This island is 12-1/2 square miles. Do people live here? _____. Long ago people lived here by making _____.

Tiny _____ is less than _____ square miles. It rises _____ feet. Only _____ ever lived here. They made _____. Does anyone live here now? _____.

The next island north is _____, also _____ at _____ square miles. No _____ live here. North of Guaguan is _____. It covers _____ square miles.

_____ rise from the ocean around the island, and there are no

_____. It is one large _____ at 2,441 feet high. It is

still _____. Do people live here? _____.

They make _____.

    The largest island north of Saipan is _____ with _____

square miles of land. The _____ built many _____,

an _____, and a _____ before World War II.

They grew _____ and _____. Pagan is the

most _____ island north of Saipan. It has towering _____

and two _____. It has _____ beaches and

_____. Until _____ over fifty people lived

here. What made them leave? _____.

_____ shot 60,000 feet into the air. The people were _____,

but no one knows when it will be _____ to return.

    The northernmost island where people live now is _____. It has

the _____ point in Micronesia, a mountain _____

feet high. There is no _____ here.

    Over fifty miles north of Agrigan lies _____. It too is

a _____ mountain rising _____ feet out of the sea.

It looks like an upside down _____ _____.

_____ is a group of _____ small islands,

East, West, and North Islands. Did anyone ever live here? _____.

Who? _____. _____ has never had people.

It is the _____ Mariana island. Many _____

nest here.

    North of the Mariana Island chain are the _____ Islands.

_____ is one. The _____ and

_____ fought a great battle here during _____.

North of these are the _____. Some people from Guam were early settlers on _____. Finally there are the large islands of _____. The Mariana, Volcano, and Bonin Islands are sometimes called "_____" to Japan. Today many Japanese like to _____ in the Mariana Islands.

Southwest of Guam are two other island chains: _____ and _____. Yap is separated from Guam by _____ miles of open _____. Yap and Palau are part of the _____. To the Southeast of Guam are the remaining Caroline Islands: _____, _____ and _____. Farther east are the _____.

## DO YOU KNOW?

1. What was copra used for?_____

_____

_____

2. How did the Japanese develop Saipan?_____

_____

_____

3. How is copra made?_____

_____

_____

**MATCHING: Match the word or place with the description.**

Agrigan                                    dried coconut meat

Aguiguan                                   first atom bombers took off from "House of Taga"

coconut oil                                developed by Japanese for sugarcane

copra                                      largest latte stones in the Marianas

Iwo Jima                                   concrete bunkers along beaches

Maug                                       comes from copra

Pagan                                      highest point in Micronesia

pillbox                                    last Chamorro battle with the Spanish was fought here

Rota                                       three small islands;  = "Guam" backwards

Saipan                                     huge World War II battle fought here

Tinian                                     an eruption like Mt. St. Helens'

# CHAPTER 9    The Fedrerated States of Micronesia (FSM)

**READING SKILLS:**

People live on _____ atolls and two single islands in the

_____ Island group. The main islands are

_____ miles southwest of Guam. Yap has about _____ square

miles of land and over _____ people. Most live on the main island.

Until recently the Yapese did not wear _____ clothes. Some men still

wear _____ and some women still wear _____.

Yap is sometimes called "the land of _____ money." It is still used in

certain kinds of _____. To buy things in a store, the Yapese use

_____. Yap's biggest town is _____. Most

people live by _____ and _____. Yap is

famous for its _____. On Ulithi Atoll people are _____

and speak a _____. On Fais Island, _____ was once

mined by the Japanese. People on the outer islands are skilled _____.

The _____ Atoll lies 600 miles southeast of Guam and has

_____ square miles of land. There are _____ main islands

with a _____ around them. There are _____

other islands in the State. People live on _____. The population is

about _____. In the past the Chuukese were known as _____,

but today they are _____.

The people in the _____ and those in the outer _____

do not speak the same _____. Almost everyone wears

_____ clothing. Most people in the capital live in _____ or

_____ houses. During _____ Japanese navy ships were bombed by the _____. Now _____ come to Chuuk to explore the _____. Today there are not enough jobs in Chuuk. Chuuk does not _____ much. Many people from Chuuk go to _____ and _____ to find jobs.

_____ lies 1,000 miles from Guam. It includes _____ coral atolls and a large _____ island. The State is _____ square miles in land area. Pohnpei is among the _____ areas in the Pacific. It gets _____ inches of _____ a year, so it is always a beautiful _____. Pohnpei is the "_____" of Micronesia. People grow _____, _____, _____, _____, _____, and _____. The _____ is the best in the world. People also make _____ items. Pohnpei exports _____ and _____.

_____ is the capital of the FSM. Many people have _____ jobs. _____ invests in Pohnpei and has a _____ here. _____ is growing too. Pohnpei State has about _____ people. They speak _____ languages: _____, _____, and _____. Some of the older people speak _____ and _____. _____ is the remains of an old temple on eighty _____ islands. The _____ of Pohnpei once lived there. Many _____ still rise over 20 feet high. Pohnpei still has a _____ system with a _____ for each district. People speak to them in a special _____. _____ was Pohnpei's first high school. Today

46

all FSM States have their own _____.

_____ is about _____ miles southeast of Pohnpei. It is a single _____ island of _____ square miles. It has a _____ history. _____ introduced disease, alcohol, and guns. In the end only a few _____ people were left. _____ also changed the Kosraeans. Today there are _____ people. Most are very _____. They are strict _____. They don't allow _____ or _____. Like Pohnpei, Kosrae gets lots of _____ and has ancient _____. People grow their own _____

## DO YOU KNOW?

1. Who was David O'Keefe and what is he famous for?_____

_____

_____

2. What is "stone money" and how do people use it?_____

_____

_____

3. Why do so many Micronesians still sail oceangoing canoes?_____

_____

_____

4. What kinds of work do people in the FSM do?_____

_____

_____

**MATCHING PUZZLE: Draw lines from the island groups to their descriptions.**

no dancing

handwoven skirts

black pepper

carved wooden love sticks

Chuuk                                          cart-wheels of stone money

Chinese investment

David O'Keefe

Kosrae                                        200 inches of rain a year

7,500 people

Japanese shipwrecks

Pohnpei                                       kings

40-mile lagoon

lost old customs

Yap                                              Mortlockese masks

Nan Madol

Protestant

thatched hotel cottages

tuna processing plant

# CHAPTER 10    Palau and the Marshall Islands

**READING SKILLS:**

Palau is a _____ archipelago. Some call it _____.

There are _____ islands and _____ square miles of land.

The biggest island is _____. Palau has _____

people who live on _____ islands. The _____

are the most beautiful, and _____ is the busiest. Included in this

_____ are the Southwest Islands of _____

and _____. The people are _____ and speak a

different language.

Some villages have a _____, a chief's _____.

Palauans carve their _____ and _____ on the

rafters. This is how the famous "_____" started.

The _____ developed these islands from 1914 until _____.

_____, _____, and _____

became important industries. Because the _____ killed many coconut

trees, people moved to _____ for work. Palauans make

_____ and _____ items. Palau is a paradise

for _____. Many people _____ in the tourist

industry. One island has _____ in the wild.

Palau has lots of _____. People farm and

_____. Many villages have their own _____

for fish. Other countries _____ to fish in Palau's waters. Palau has many

successful _____ people. _____ is one.

Palauan people value_____.

The _____ is the farthest from Guam. It is _____ miles from Guam to the capital at _____. There are_____ Marshallese on _____ atoll islands. The land area totals _____ square miles. All the islands are _____ and _____. Most are less than a square _____. The Marshall Islands is spread out over _____ miles. The Marshallese are famous for their "_____" for navigation. The Marshallese were once known as _____. The _____ stopped their tribal wars in the early 1900s. Most are of the _____ religion.

The _____ used some of the Marshall Islands for _____. Americans tested _____ bombs on _____ Atoll and _____ Atoll. These islands are still _____. _____ is a Pacific Missile Range Facility. The U.S. military fires missiles from _____.

The Marshallese raise _____, _____, _____, and _____, but sometimes there is not enough _____. They _____ and sell _____, _____, _____, and _____. Many people live in _____ and work for the _____ or _____. Majuro has a _____ plant. The fish are sold to _____.

## MATCHING: Match the name or thing with its description.

Airai Hotel                     low and narrow

bai                             Palau

"Ejoij ke"                      owns Pacific Development Corporation

Enewetak                        keep monkeys as pets

ice plants                      chief's meeting house

Marshall Islands                Villages in Palau have these.

Palau                           Is he kind?

Palauans                        for navigation

Roman Tmetuchl                  Japan developed it from 1914.

stick charts                    radioactive

## DO YOU KNOW?

1. How did the Palauan "storyboard" start?_____

_____

_____

2. How did monkeys get to Palau?_____

_____

_____

3. Why is Palau a popular tourist spot?_____

_____

_____

4. Why can't people move back to Bikini Atoll?_____

_____

_____


5. Describe "stick charts" and explain how they were used._____

_____

_____